The Complete Instant Pot Cookbook For Beginners

Step By Step Easy Pressure Cooker Recipes Anyone Can Cook and Enjoy Delicious Meals at home

Colleen Williams

© Copyright 2021 - All rights reserved.

ISBN: 9798595830010

The contents of this book may not be reproduced, duplicated or transmitted without direct written permission from the author.

Under no circumstances will any legal responsibility or blame be held against the publisher for any reparation, damages, or monetary loss due to the information herein, either directly or indirectly.

Legal Notice:

This book is copyright protected. This is only for personal use. You cannot amend, distribute, sell, use, quote or paraphrase any part of the content within this book without the consent of the author.

Disclaimer Notice:

Please note the information contained within this document is for educational and entertainment purposes only. Every attempt has been made to provide accurate, up to date and reliable information. No warranties of any kind are expressed or implied. Readers acknowledge that the author is not engaging in the rendering of legal, financial, medical or professional advice. The content of this book has been derived from various sources. Please consult a licensed professional before attempting any techniques outlined in this book.

By reading this document, the reader agrees that under no circumstances are is the author responsible for any losses, direct or indirect, which are incurred as a result of the use of information contained within this document, including, but not limited to, —errors, omissions, or inaccuracies.

Table of Contents

Introduction 5

Chapter 1: The Instant Pot Explained 6

Chapter 2: Beef   Recipes 20 11

Chapter 3: Fish and Sea Food 38

Chapter 4: Poultry   Recipes 69

Chapter 5: Vegan Recipes 96

Chapter 6: Soup & Stew Recipes 113

Chapter 7: Rice Recipes 129

Chapter 8: Pasta Recipes 135

Chapter 9: Dessert Recipes 143

Conclusion 150

Do you want to cook healthy meals?

Do you want save on your kitchen space?

Do you want to revolutionize your cooking?

If you answered yes to any of these questions, keep reading to know more.
Do you want to cook healthy meals? Do you want save on your kitchen space? Do you want to revolutionize your cooking? If you answered yes to any of these questions, keep reading to know more.

You can easily cook delicious and healthy meals with the Instant Pot. This amazing cooking pot helps you save on your power bill because it takes less time to cook meals. If you are looking for recipes that can be prepared quickly, then this book is designed specifically for you. This book will help you discover the secret behind making delicious meals in the Instant Pot pressure cooker.
Inside, you will find recipes for every type of meal you can think of. That's not all! The Instant Pot Cookbook also tells you about the best ways to use your Instant Pot. You will find a large number of tips and methods that can help you prepare delicious meals more quickly than ever before.
The recipe categories in this book are as follows:
- Beef
- Fish and sea food
- Poultry
- Vegan
- Soup and stews
- Rice
- Pasta
- Dessert

Get yourself this book and start your journey with the Instant Pot.
Happy cooking!

Introduction

The Instant Pot has revolutionized cooking in this modern era. The Instant Pot can cook meals that require long cooking times at high pressure, while bringing the ingredients to temperature faster than on stove top.

This Cookbook contains a collection of 100 easy-to-make recipes that can make anyone into a good cook. The recipes are divided into different categories to make them easier for you to follow.

For beginners, the best idea is to follow the instructions to the letter. Read this cookbook carefully and thoroughly, as it contains easy-to-follow instructions for preparing tasty meals in accordance with your preferences.

Happy cooking!

Master The Art Of Instant Pot Cooking

Chapter 1: The Instant Pot Explained

The Instant Pot is a modern electric pressure cooker that allows you to cook a variety of dishes in no time at all. It features a simple and intuitive control panel with digital timer and temperature settings. The Instant Pot is easy to use and clean, the lid features a small and removable pot-in-pot that can be used as a steam tray. The Instant Pot can cook meals that require long cooking times at high pressure, while bringing the ingredients to temperature faster than on stove top. The device also has a sauté setting that lets you brown foods such as onions or garlic before pressure cooking without dirtying another dish.

Advantages of the Instant Pot

No-burn

The Instant Pot pressure cooker does not burn food due to its high temperature setting which is different from typical cooking pots. The steam created in the high temperature environment of the pot allows for quick cooking of ingredients under pressure. However, the pot prevents burning when it comes into contact with food during cooking.

Easy to use

A pressure cooker is a unique cooking device. It is not like others that you can just plug in and start cooking. Most traditional pressure cookers are somewhat difficult to use which is why it was not very popular in the past. But the instant pot is different, even a beginner can easily use the device while having fun doing so. It is also safe to use for children, as there are no hot surfaces and few parts to play with.

Safe

The pressure cooker uses a pressure sensing system, it knows when it's time to release the pressure and stops working. The pressure cooker has a built-in device that senses the proper cooking pressure and shuts off automatically once the indicator turns red. There is also another safety feature called the Automatic Keep Warm feature that is designed in case of power outage or sudden stoppage of cooking process.

High Quality

The Instant Pot is made from high quality stainless steel. The pressure cooker has an aluminum insert, a stainless steel lid and handles. The interior is made from aluminum that is non-reactive in the cooking process. The lid also features a removable pot-in-pot that can be used as a steam tray. It also comes with an accessory kit that makes it easy to use and clean required tools for cleaning the device.

Functionality

The Instant Pot is easy to use as it allows you to do all sorts of cooking ranging from pressure cooker, rice cooker, yogurt maker and slow cooker. It also has a sauté setting that is designed for meats and vegetables before pressure cooking without adding more ingredients. The device has temperature settings ranging from high up to low for cooking.

Easy to clean

The pot and lid of the instant pot are dishwasher safe, while the base and side handles can be cleaned in the sink with a small brush. The device also comes with an accessory kit that allows you to clean all the tools needed for cleaning for your Instant Pot.

Sizes

The Instant Pot comes in two sizes; 6 quart and 8 quart. The device is also available in an additional capacity of 8 quart plus model that is designed for larger meals. The smaller one is useful for 4-6 people while the larger ones are for 6-8 people. There is also a 7-in-1 programmable multi cooker that has been designed to replace other kitchen appliances including rice cooker, pressure cooker, slow cooker, yogurt maker, sauté/browning, steamer and warmer. This additional function gives the device an edge over others.

Close to zero power loss

Instant Pot engineers used high-quality stainless steel and insulation material to build Instant Pot. Also if you look at the device's heating plate, you will notice that it is made of stainless steel. Another advantage of using stainless steel in the device is that it is resistant to getting rusty and gives a better cooking experience.

Durability

The Instant Pot is built with high quality stainless steel that does not get corroded easily. The stainless steel lid also ensures that no bacteria or dangerous microbes can enter your food. The whole device is built to last. Although it is quite costly, it's worth the price. Even if you are not a pressure cooker lover, you will realize the joy of cooking in a pressure cooker after you use this Instant Pot.

Functions of the Instant Pot

Meat/Stew: With this Instant Pot setting, you can prepare Paleo meat or stew recipes. It's default cooking time is set at high pressure for 35 minutes.

Soup: With this Instant Pot setting, you can prepare various Paleo soup recipes. It's default cooking time is set at high pressure for 30 minutes.

Cake: This setting is for making a variety of cakes.

Keep Warm/Cancel: With this Instant Pot setting, you can cancel any program that has been previously set. This setting puts the cooker in standby.

Steam: This setting lets your steam seafood, and veggies. It also reheats foods. It's default cooking time is set at high pressure for 10 minutes.

Poultry: With this Instant Pot setting, you can prepare various poultry recipes. It's default cooking time is set at high pressure for 15 minutes.

Bean/Chili: This setting is for making chili or cooking beans. It's default cooking time is set at high pressure for 30 minutes.

Yogurt: The default of this setting is 8 hours of incubation time. You can use "Adjust" to increase or decrease cooking time.

Sauté: With this Instant Pot setting, you can do open lid browning, sautéing or simmering of added ingredients usually onions, garlic, etc.

Egg: With this Instant Pot setting, you can make variety of egg-based recipes.

Manual: This setting lets you manually set your own pressure and cooking time.

Slow Cook: Many recipes call for slow cooking, which takes many hours to cook added ingredients slowly. This setting converts your Instant Pot into a slow cooker. It can cook to up to 40 hours. It's default cooking time is set at high pressure for 4 hours.

Safety Features:

Compared to traditional pressure cookers, the Instant Pot is designed to avoid potential problems thus you can ensure your safety every time you cook food. Below are the safety features of this intuitive electric pressure cooker.

Pressure regulation: It is important to take note that the Instant Pot has an operating pressure of 11.6 PSI. Once the inner pot exceeds this pressure, it will release steam automatically to maintain a stable pressure. But what if this feature malfunctions? The Instant Pot has an internal protection mechanism that shifts the inner pot downward to create a gap so that it can accommodate high pressure, but this rarely happens in real life.

Anti-blocking vent: Small particles of food can find their way into the steam vent and can jam it over time thus making it difficult to release pressure and steam. The Instant Pot has a vent shield that prevents food particles from clogging the vent.

Lid close detection: This feature ensures that the lid is properly closed and sealed before cooking. If the lid is not closed properly, the Instant Pot does not activate pressurized cooking and you are only allowed to use the "Sauté" and "Keep Warm" buttons.

Temperature control: The Instant Pot has a built-in thermostat found just under the inner pot. This thermostat is responsible for controlling the temperature to a safe range based on the pre-set temperature of the setting chosen.

Leaky lid protection: Referring to leaking lids, this safety features measures the pre-heating time as well as detect the pressure changes within the inner pot. The presence of leaks results in the inability of the Instant Pot to build enough pressure thus it will just switch to the "Keep Warm" function instead of the pre-set button that you selected.

Chapter 2: Beef Recipes 20

Milk-Braised Beef Loin

Prep Time: 10 minutes
Cooking Time: 1 hour
Servings: 4

Ingredients:
- 1 2-pound beef loin roast
- 1 teaspoon salt
- ½ teaspoon black pepper
- 2 tablespoons olive oil
- 2 tablespoons butter
- 3 cups whole milk
- 1 onion, sliced
- 3 cloves garlic, peeled

Directions:
1. Season the beef with salt and pepper. Heat the oil and butter in the Instant Pot on Sauté mode. Brown the beef on all sides.

2. Pour in milk, plus more to cover if necessary. Arrange onions and garlic around the beef. Close lid and set cooking time for 60 minutes on high pressure. Use quick release to remove the steam.
3. Transfer beef to a serving dish. Pour sauce into a blender and blend until smooth. Pour back into Instant Pot and set to Sauté mode. Reduce to your desired consistency and season to taste with salt and pepper.
4. Serve sauce over pork.

Nutritional Value Per Serving:
Calories 663
Fat 38.52 g
Carbohydrates 9.95 g
Protein 66.02 g

Chicken Ragout

Prep Time: 10 minutes
Cooking Time: 15 minutes
Servings: 4
Ingredients:

- 2 tablespoons olive oil
- 4 chicken thighs
- 1 onion, diced
- 1 clove garlic, minced
- 1 teaspoon thyme
- ½ teaspoon rosemary
- 1 tablespoon tomato paste
- 1 cup red wine
- 2 cups chicken stock
- 1 bay leaf
- ½ teaspoon salt
- ½ teaspoon black pepper

Directions:
1. Set Instant Pot to Sauté and oil. Brown chicken thighs in hot oil; remove to a plate.
2. Add onion and garlic and cook until onion is translucent, then add thyme and rosemary and cook 30 seconds. Add tomato sauce and cook an additional 30 seconds. Pour in the wine and deglaze the pan, then add chicken stock, bay leaf, salt, and pepper. Place chicken back in the pot.
3. Close the lid and set cooking time for 10 minutes on high pressure. Serve with crusty bread.

Nutritional Value Per Serving:
Calories 522
Fat 39.14 g
Carbohydrates 5.07 g
Protein 33.28 g

Chop Suey

Prep Time: 5 minutes
Cooking Time: 15 minutes
Servings: 4

Ingredients:
- 1 tablespoon olive oil
- ½ pound ground beef
- 1 onion, diced
- 2 cloves garlic, minced
- 1 can whole tomatoes in their juice, crushed
- ½ cup beef stock
- 1 tablespoon Worcestershire sauce
- ½ teaspoon salt
- ½ teaspoon black pepper
- ½ pound uncooked macaroni
- 1 cup shredded mozzarella cheese

Directions:
1. Heat olive oil in Instant Pot on Saute mode. Brown beef and drain excess fat, then add onions and garlic.
2. Pour in tomatoes, stock, Worcestershire, salt, and pepper. Stir in pasta and half of the cheese.

3. Close lid and set cooking time to 8 minutes on high pressure. Use quick release to remove steam.
4. Sprinkle the remaining cheese over the pasta and close lid until the cheese is melted. Serve.

Nutritional Value Per Serving:
Calories 495
Fat 19.89 g
Carbohydrates 48.74 g
Protein 29.07 g

Game Day Buffalo Wings

Prep Time: 5 minutes
Cooking Time: 5 minutes
Servings: 4
Ingredients:
- 2 pounds chicken wings
- 1 teaspoon salt
- 1 teaspoon black pepper
- 2/3 cup hot sauce
- ½ cup butter
- 1 tablespoon apple cider vinegar
- ¼ teaspoon Worcestershire sauce
- 1 garlic clove, minced
- ½ cup water

Directions:
1. Season the chicken wings with salt and pepper.
2. Combine hot sauce, butter, vinegar, Worcestershire sauce, garlic, and water in the Instant Pot. Put the steamer basket in place and arrange the wings in it.
3. Close the lid and set cooking time for 5 minutes. Use quick release to remove the steam.
4. Remove the steamer basket with the wings. Set the pot to Saute mode and reduce the sauce to your desired consistency.
5. Toss the wings with the sauce and serve with blue cheese dressing.

Nutritional Value Per Serving:
Calories 498
Fat 31.36 g
Carbohydrates 1.14 g
Protein 50.69 g

Texas Chicken Tamales

Prep Time: 30 minutes

Cooking Time: 25 minutes
Servings: 6
Ingredients:
- 3 cups masa flour
- 1 teaspoon salt
- 1 teaspoon baking powder
- 1 cup olive oil
- 2 cups chicken stock
- ½ teaspoon black pepper
- 1 pack corn husks, rinsed and soaked
- 2 cups cooked, shredded chicken
- 1 can chipotle sauce
- 1 cup shredded Mexican cheese

Directions:
1. In a bowl, mix together flour, salt, and baking powder, then stir in oil and stock.
2. In a separate bowl, mix together chicken and chipotle sauce.
3. Place about ¼ cup of masa mixture on a corn husk and shape into a log. Layer 2 tablespoons of chicken over the mass, followed by an equal amount of cheese. Roll the husk into a tube and fold down the ends. Repeat with the remaining corn husks.
4. Pour 1 cup of water into the Instant Pot and set the steamer basket in place. Arrange the tamales in the basket. Close the lid and set the cooking time for 25 minutes on high.

Nutritional Value Per Serving:
Calories 800
Fat 43.46 g
Carbohydrates 34.49 g
Protein 66.32 g

Chicken Marsala

Prep Time: 5 minutes
Cooking Time: 15 minutes
Servings: 4
Ingredients:
- 4 chicken thighs
- ½ teaspoon salt
- ½ teaspoon black pepper
- 1 tablespoon olive oil
- 1 tablespoon butter
- 1 onion, finely chopped
- 1 garlic clove, minced
- 1 cup mushrooms, sliced
- 1 teaspoon thyme
- ½ teaspoon rosemary
- 2 tablespoons flour
- 2 cups chicken stock
- ½ cup marsala wine

Directions:

1. Season chicken thighs with salt and pepper. Set Instant Pot to Sauté and add olive oil. Brown chicken on both sides, then removes to a plate.
2. Add butter to pot. When melted, add onion and garlic. When the onion is translucent, add mushrooms and cook until tender. Add thyme and rosemary and cook 30 seconds.
3. Stir flour into the pot and cook about 1 minute or until the flour begins to take on color. Add wine, stirring constantly, and deglaze the pot. Stir in chicken stock and wine. Replace chicken in the pot.
4. Close the lid and set cooking time for 10 minutes on high.
5. Serve with pasta or crusty bread.

Nutritional Value Per Serving:

Calories 534
Fat 38.17 g
Carbohydrates 11.18 g
Protein 24g

Creamy Chicken and Rice Casserole

Prep Time: 5 minutes
Cooking Time: 10 minutes

Servings: 4
Ingredients:
- 1 pound boneless chicken, cubed
- ½ teaspoon salt
- ½ teaspoon black pepper
- 1 can cream of chicken soup
- 1 cup water
- 1 onion, finely chopped
- 1 teaspoon dried thyme
- 3/4 cup uncooked rice
- 2 cups broccoli florets, chopped small
- ½ cup shredded Cheddar cheese

Directions:
1. Season the chicken with salt and pepper. Place in instant pot with soup, water, onion, thyme, rice, broccoli, and cheese.
2. Close lid and set cooking time for 10 minutes. Allow steam to release naturally. Serve.

Nutritional Value Per Serving:
Calories 362
Fat 17.14 g
Carbohydrates 25.21 g
Protein 33.26 g

Traditional Beef Stew

Prep time: 15 minutes
Cooking Time: 35 minutes
Servings: 2

Ingredients:
- 1lb diced stewing steak
- 1lb chopped vegetables
- 1 cup low sodium beef broth
- 1tbsp black pepper

Directions:
1. Mix all the ingredients in your Instant Pot.
2. Cook on Stew for 35 minutes. Release the pressure naturally.

Nutritional Value Per Serving:
Calories 222g
Fat 14.5 Fiber 0.2g
Carbs 0.8g
Protein 20.9g

Minced Beef

Prep time: 15 minutes
Cooking Time: 35 minutes
Servings: 2
Ingredients:
- 1.5lb lean steak, minced
- 1 cup low sodium gravy
- 2tbsp mixed spices

Directions:
1. Mix all the ingredients in your Instant Pot.
2. Cook on Stew for 35 minutes.
3. Release the pressure naturally.
4. Serve and enjoy.

Nutritional Value Per Serving:
Calories: 200
Carbs: 2 g
Fat: 5 g
Protein: 48g

Thai Coconut Beef

Prep time: 5 minutes
Cooking Time: 40 minutes
Servings: 5
Ingredients:
- 3 tablespoons toasted sesame seed oil
- 2 cloves of garlic
- 1 teaspoon ginger, sliced
- 1-pound beef, sliced into strips
- 1 cup coconut milk, freshly squeezed

Directions:
1. Press the "Sauté" button on the Instant Pot and heat the oil.
2. Sauté the garlic and ginger until fragrant.
3. Add the beef and stir for a minute.
4. Pour in the coconut milk and season with salt and pepper to taste.
5. Close the lid and make sure that the vent points to "Sealing."
6. Press the "Meat/Stew" button and adjust the time to 40 minutes.

7. Do quick pressure release

Nutritional Value Per Serving:
Calories 311
Carbohydrates: 5.1g
Protein: 28.1g
Fat: 14.7g

Beef Brisket

Prep time: 5 minutes
Cooking Time: 66 minutes
Servings: 8
Ingredients:
- 2 ½ pounds of beef brisket
- ¼ of a cup of BBQ sauce or seasoning
- 4 slices of white onion, peeled
- 2 tablespoons of apple cider vinegar
- 2 tablespoons of low sugar ketchup

Directions:
1. Cover the brisket thoroughly with BBQ sauce (or seasoning)

2. Set your instant pot to sauté and drizzle in some mild tasting cooking oil. Put the brisket in and sear on both sides – 3-4 minutes per side.
3. Take the brisket out using tongs. Place the onion slices at the bottom of the cooker and put the brisket back on top of them. Remember to place the fat side up.
4. Thoroughly mix together the apple cider vinegar, ketchup and water, then pour it around the meat.
5. Close the lid and the vent, choose the manual setting and cook under high pressure for 60 minutes.
6. Once it's done, quickly release the pressure and steam and carefully open the lid. Transfer the brisket to a cutting board and let it rest for 10-15 minutes. Then, slice the meat and serve with the jus from the cooker and the onions.

Nutritional Value Per Serving:
Calories: 385
Fat: 27 g
Carb: 2 g
Proteins: 30 g

Beef Stroganoff

Prep time: 5 minutes
Cooking Time: 30 minutes
Servings: 4
Ingredients:
- 3 tablespoons butter
- 3 cloves of garlic minced
- 1-pound beef stew meat, cut into strips
- ½ cup heavy cream
- 2 tablespoon lemon juice, freshly squeezed

Directions:
1. Press the "Sauté" button on the Instant Pot and heat the butter.
2. Sauté the garlic until fragrant.
3. Stir in the beef for 2 minutes.
4. Add water and season with salt and pepper to taste.
5. Pour in the heavy cream.
6. Close the lid and make sure that the vent points to "Sealing."
7. Press the "Meat/Stew" button and adjust the time to 30 minutes.
8. Do quick pressure release.
9. Once the lid is open, garnish with lemon juice and parsley.

Nutritional Value Per Serving:
Calories 226
Carbohydrates: 1.3g
Protein:29.9g
Fat: 30.7g

Sesame Beef

Prep time: 5 minutes
Cooking Time: 33 minutes
Servings: 4
Ingredients:
- 2 tablespoons coconut oil
- 1-pound ribeye steak, cut into strips
- 1 red pepper, seeded and julienned
- 1 thumb-sized ginger, sliced
- 2 tablespoons sesame oil or toasted sesame seeds

Directions:
1. Press the "Sauté" button on the Instant Pot and stir the beef, red pepper, and ginger.
2. Season with salt and pepper to taste.
3. Pour in ¾ cup of water.

4. Close the lid and make sure that the vent points to "Sealing."
5. Press the "Meat/Stew" button and adjust the time to 30 minutes.
6. Do quick pressure release.
7. Garnish with sesame seeds or sesame oil.

Nutritional Value Per Serving:
Calories 298
Carbohydrates: 4.1g
Protein: 21.7g
Fat: 22.9g

Ground Beef Stir Fry

Prep time: 5 minutes
Cooking Time: 45 minutes
Servings: 2
Ingredients:
- 5 tablespoons coconut oil
- 3 cloves of garlic, minced
- ½ onion, chopped
- 1-pound ground beef

- 2 green bell peppers, seeded and diced

Directions:
1. Press the "Sauté" button on the Instant Pot and heat the coconut oil.
2. Sauté the garlic and onions until fragrant.
3. Stir in the ground beef and season with salt and pepper to taste.
4. Pour a cup of water.
5. Close the lid and make sure that the vent points to "Sealing."
6. Press the "Meat/Stew" button and adjust the time to 35 minutes.
7. Do quick pressure release.
8. Once the lid is open, press the "Sauté" button and stir in the bell pepper.
9. Allow to simmer for 5 minutes.

Nutritional Value Per Serving:
Calories 937
Carbohydrates: 15.8g
Protein: 59.7g
Fat: 71.1g

Sirloin Beef Roast

Prep time: 5 minutes
Cooking Time: 1 hour and 40 minutes
Servings: 8

Ingredients:
- 4 tablespoons olive oil
- 1 beef sirloin roast
- 1 onion, quartered
- 2 tablespoons oregano
- 1 ½ teaspoon chili pepper flakes

Directions:
1. Press the "Sauté" button on the Instant Pot and heat the olive oil.
2. Sear the roast on all edges.
3. Add the rest of the ingredients and allow to sauté for 2 minutes.
4. Pour a cup of water and season with salt and pepper to taste.
5. Close the lid and make sure that the vent points to "Sealing."
6. Press the "Meat/Stew" button and adjust the time to 1 hour and 30 minutes.
7. Do quick pressure release.

Nutritional Value Per Serving:
Calories 203
Carbohydrates: 1.3g

Protein: 13.5g
Fat: 18.2g

Mexican Shredded Beef

Prep time: 5 minutes
Cooking Time: 12 hours
Servings: 12
Ingredients:
- 5 tablespoons olive oil
- 4 cloves of garlic
- 3-pound beef chuck roast
- 1 teaspoon ground cumin
- 2 tablespoons liquid smoke

Directions:
1. Place all ingredients in the Instant Pot and season with salt and pepper to taste.
2. Pour a cup of water.
3. Close the lid and make sure that the vent points to "Venting."
4. Press the "Slow Cook" button and adjust the time to 12 hours.

5. Once cooked, shred the beef using two forks.

Nutritional Value Per Serving:
Calories 259
Carbohydrates: 0.4g
Protein: 20.4g
Fat: 25.6g

Korean Ground Beef

Prep time: 15 minutes
Cooking Time: 25 minutes
Servings: 6
Ingredients:
- 1 tablespoon of extra-virgin olive oil
- 1 ½ pound of ground beef
- 2 teaspoons of garlic powder
- 1 teaspoon of ground ginger
- 1 teaspoon of dried minced onions
- ½ cup of homemade low-sodium beef broth
- ¼ cup of coconut aminos
- 1 teaspoon of sriracha sauce
- Fine sea salt and freshly cracked black pepper (to taste)

Directions:

1. Press the "Sauté" setting on your Instant Pot and add the olive oil. Once hot, add the ground beef and cook until brown, breaking apart the meat with a wooden spoon.
2. Add the remaining ingredients and lock the lid. Cook at high pressure for 7 minutes. When the cooking is done, naturally release the pressure for 5 minutes, then quick release the remaining pressure. Carefully remove the lid.
3. Press the "Sauté" setting on your Instant Pot and continue to cook until most of the liquid reduces.
4. Serve and enjoy!

Nutritional Value Per Serving:
Calories: 210
Fat: 10g
Carbs: 6g
Protein: 22g

Ground Beef Stir-Fry

Prep time: 15 minutes
Cooking Time: 20 minutes
Servings: 4
Ingredients:
- 1 pound of ground beef
- 2 green bell peppers, seeds removed and finely chopped
- 3 medium tomatoes, finely chopped
- ½ medium onion, finely chopped
- 2 medium garlic cloves, peeled and minced
- ¼ cup of fresh cilantro, chopped
- 1 teaspoon of hot sauce
- 2 tablespoons of coconut oil
- Fine sea salt and freshly cracked black pepper (to taste)

Directions:
1. Press the "Sauté" setting on your Instant Pot. Once hot, add the ground beef and cook until brown, breaking up the meat with a wooden spoon. Remove and set aside.
2. Add the coconut oil. Once hot, add the chopped onions, tomatoes, peppers inside your Instant Pot. Cook for 5 minutes, stirring frequently.

3. Return the ground beef to the pot and continue to cook until the vegetables have softened, stir in the hot sauce, cilantro, coconut oil, minced garlic, sea salt and freshly cracked black pepper.
4. Serve and enjoy!

Nutritional Value Per Serving:
Calories: 313
Fat: 14.2g
Carbs: 6g
Protein: 36.1g

Beef Hot Dogs

Prep Time: 10 min
Cooking Time: 4 min
Servings: 2
Ingredients:
- 1/3 tablespoon cider vinegar
- 2 beef sausages, cured, cooked and smoked
- 1 cup fresh water
- 2 buns
- 1/3 teaspoon ground cumin

Directions:

1. Put the vinegar, ground cumin, beef sausages, and water in the 3-quart Instant Pot Mini.
2. Fasten the lid and cook on high pressure for 4 minutes.
3. Once the Instant Pot Mini comes to pressure, then the selected cook time will begin.
4. Naturally release the pressure and shift the sausages in a platter.
5. Put the sausages in between the buns and serve warm.

Nutritional Values Per Serving:
Calories: 132
Fat: 6g
Carbohydrates: 14.5g
Protein: 4.5g

Buttered Beef

Prep time: 10 minutes
Cooking Time: 1 hour
Servings: 6
Ingredients:
- 3 pounds of beef roast
- 2 tablespoons of ranch dressing seasoning
- 1 1-pint jar of drained pepper rings (reserve ¼ of a cup of the liquid)
- 2 tablespoon of zesty Italian seasoning

- 1 whole stick of butter

Directions:
1. Drizzle a little light cooking oil (vegetable works best) and set your cooker to sautéing. Once it's hot, brown the roast on each side.
2. Turn the instant pot off and add 1 cup of water, the seasonings, pepper rings and the pepper juice you saved onto the roast. Finish by placing the whole stick of butter on top of the meat.
3. Close the lid of the pot and seal the valve. Using the manual setting, set the time for 60 minutes. If your roast is larger than 3 pounds, you may need to extend the time up to 90 minutes.
4. After the cooking is done, you can quickly release the pressure or let it drop naturally. Give the roast a bit of time to rest and slice it or shred it using two forks. Serve with your preferred side dishes.

Nutritional Value Per Serving:
Calories: 859
Carbohydrate: 6.4 g
Proteins: 31.5 g
Fat: 79 g

Chapter 3: Fish and Sea Food

Glazed Salmon

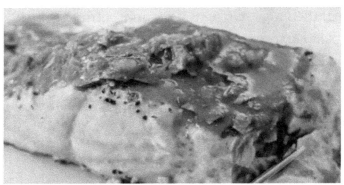

Prep Time: 20 min
Cooking Time: 11 min
Servings: 2

Ingredients:
- ¼ cup white wine
- 2 (6 oz.) salmon steaks
- ½ tablespoon low sodium soy sauce
- 1 tablespoon balsamic vinegar
- 1 tablespoon maple syrup
- ¼ teaspoon lemon pepper seasoning

Directions:
1. Marinate the salmon with wine, soy sauce, maple syrup, balsamic vinegar, and lemon pepper seasoning.
2. Put the marinated salmon in the 3-quart Instant Pot Mini.
3. Fasten the lid and cook on high pressure for 8 minutes.
4. Once the Instant Pot Mini comes to pressure, then the selected cook time will begin.
5. Naturally release the pressure and shift the salmon steaks to a platter.

6. Press "sauté" and sauté the sauce for 3 minutes.
7. Top the salmon steaks with the sauce and serve hot.

Nutritional Value Per Serving:
Calories: 280
Fat: 10.5g
Carbohydrates: 8.1g
Protein: 33.3g

Steamed Clams

Prep Time: 10 min
Cooking Time: 5 min
Servings: 3

Ingredients:
- 1/8 cup butter, melted
- ¼ cup white wine
- 1 pound mushy shell clams
- 1 teaspoon garlic powder
- ¼ cup fresh lemon juice

Directions:
1. Combine the butter with white wine, garlic powder and lemon juice.

2. Place a trivet in the 3-quart Instant Pot Mini and pour in the white wine mixture.
3. Put the clams on the trivet and fasten the lid.
4. Cook on high pressure for 3 minutes.
5. Once the Instant Pot Mini comes to pressure, then the selected cook time will begin.
6. Naturally release the pressure and shift the clams in a platter.
7. Top with the remaining dressing and serve hot.

Nutritional Value Per Serving:
Calories: 204
Fat: 9.3g
Carbohydrates: 5.6g
Protein: 19.7g

Sherry Cod

Prep Time: 15 min
Cooking Time: 9 min
Servings: 2
Ingredients:
- 1 tablespoon maple syrup
- ¼ cup sherry

- ¼ teaspoon lemon pepper seasoning
- ½ tablespoon soy sauce
- 2 (6 oz.) cod steaks
- 1 tablespoon balsamic vinegar

Directions:
1. Marinate the cod steaks with sherry, soy sauce, maple syrup, balsamic vinegar, and lemon pepper seasoning.
2. Put the marinated salmon in the 3-quart Instant Pot Mini.
3. Fasten the lid and cook on high pressure for 6 minutes.
4. Once the Instant Pot Mini comes to pressure, then the selected cook time will begin.
5. Naturally release the pressure and shift the salmon steaks to a platter.
6. Press "SAUTÉ" and sauté the sauce for 3 minutes.
7. Top the cod steaks with the sauce and serve hot.

Nutritional Value Per Serving:
Calories: 216
Fat: 1.5g
Carbohydrates: 7.3g
Protein: 39.1g

Cheesy Tilapia

Prep Time: 15 min
Cooking Time: 10 min
Servings: 2

Ingredients:
- ½ cup Parmesan cheese, grated
- 2 tilapia fillets
- 1/8 cup mayonnaise
- Salt and black pepper, to taste
- 1/8 cup fresh lemon juice

Directions:
1. Marinate the tilapia fillets with fresh lemon juice, mayonnaise, salt, and black pepper.
2. Put the marinated tilapia in the 3-quart Instant Pot Mini.
3. Fasten the lid and cook on high pressure for 7 minutes.
4. Once the Instant Pot Mini comes to pressure, then the selected cook time will begin.
5. Naturally release the pressure and stir in the Parmesan cheese.
6. Press "Sauté" and sauté for 3 minutes.
7. Shift the contents of the Instant Pot Mini in a bowl and serve with your favorite side dish.

Nutritional Value Per Serving:
Calories: 244
Fat: 12.1g
Carbohydrates: 4.9g
Protein: 30.3g

Sweet and Sour Fish

Prep Time: 10 min
Cooking Time: 9 min
Servings: 3
Ingredients:
- ½ tablespoon sugar
- 1 pound fish, chunked
- ½ tablespoon olive oil
- 1 tablespoon soy sauce
- 1 tablespoon vinegar
- Salt and black pepper, to taste

Directions:
1. Put the olive oil and fish chunks in the 3-quart Instant Pot Mini.
2. Select "Sauté" and sauté for 3 minutes.
3. Stir in the sugar, soy sauce, vinegar, salt, and black pepper.
4. Fasten the lid and cook on high pressure for 6 minutes.
5. Once the Instant Pot Mini comes to pressure, then the selected cook time will begin.
6. Naturally release the pressure and shift the contents of the Instant Pot Mini in a platter.
7. Serve hot.

Nutritional Value Per Serving:
Calories: 231
Fat: 11.7g

Carbohydrates: 2.5g
Protein: 29.7g

Clams with Béchamel Sauce

Prep Time: 10 min
Cooking Time: 4 min
Servings: 3

Ingredients:
- ¼ cup red wine
- 3 tablespoons olive oil
- 1 pound shell clams
- ¼ cup fresh lemon juice
- 1 teaspoon ginger powder
- ½ cup béchamel sauce

Directions:
1. Combine the butter with red wine, ginger powder and lemon juice.
2. Place a trivet in the 3-quart Instant Pot Mini and pour in the red wine mixture.
3. Put the shell clams on the trivet and fasten the lid.
4. Cook on high pressure for 4 minutes.

5. Once the Instant Pot Mini comes to pressure, then the selected cook time will begin.
6. Naturally release the pressure and shift the clams in a platter.
7. Top with the béchamel sauce and serve hot.

Nutritional Value Per Serving:
Calories: 269
Fat: 16.4g
Carbohydrates: 6.7g
Protein: 20.2g

Saffron Prawns

Prep Time: 15 min
Cooking Time: 13 min
Servings: 3

Ingredients:
- 2 tablespoons butter
- ½ cup seafood inventory
- 1 lemon juice and zest
- 1/3 cup parmesan cheese
- 6 large prawns, peeled and deveined
- 1 onion, chopped

- 1 tablespoon garlic, minced
- 1½ cups chicken broth
- 6 saffron strands emulsified in water

Directions:
1. Put the butter and prawns in the 3-quart Instant Pot Mini.
2. Select "SAUTÉ" and sauté for 3 minutes.
3. Stir in the garlic and onions and sauté for 2 minutes.
4. Add the seafood inventory, saffron emulsion, chicken broth, lemon zest, and juice.
5. Fasten the lid and cook on high pressure for 8 minutes.
6. Once the Instant Pot Mini comes to pressure, then the selected cook time will begin.
7. Naturally release the pressure and shift the contents of the Instant Pot Mini in a platter.
8. Serve hot.

Nutritional Value Per Serving:
Calories: 182
Fat: 12.2g
Carbohydrates: 7.9g
Protein: 11.5g

Seafood Paella

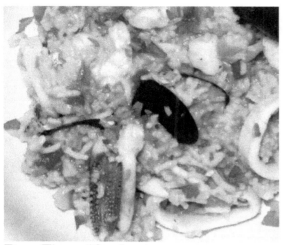

Prep Time: 10 minutes
Cooking Time: 10 minutes
Servings: 4

Ingredients:
- 1 tablespoon olive oil
- ½ pound chorizo
- 1 onion, chopped
- 1 red bell pepper, chopped
- 2 garlic cloves, minced
- 1 pinch saffron
- 2 teaspoons dried thyme
- 2/3 cup rice
- 1 pound whole shrimp
- 2 tablespoons tomato paste
- 1/3 cup stock or water
- ½ teaspoon salt
- ½ teaspoon black pepper

Directions:
1. Set Instant Pot to Sauté mode. Add oil, then brown chorizo.

2. Add onion and bell pepper and cook until onion is translucent, then add garlic, saffron, and thyme. Cook until fragrant.
3. Add rice and toast until grains become opaque.
4. Add tomato paste and shrimp and toss until shrimp are well-coated with seasonings. Pour in stock or water, salt, and pepper.
5. Close lid. Set cooking time to 6 minutes on high pressure.

Nutritional Value Per Serving:
Calories 54
Fat 25. 94 g
Carbohydrates 33.59 g
Protein 33.59 g

Cape Cod Lobster Bake

Prep Time: 10 minutes
Cooking Time: 10 minutes
Servings: 4
Ingredients:
- 6 cups water
- 2 tablespoons Old Bay
- 1 tablespoon paprika
- 1 teaspoon salt
- 1 onion, quartered
- 3 cloves garlic, peeled
- 3 sprigs thyme
- 2 bay leaves
- 1 pound small red potatoes, halved
- ½ pound chorizo, sliced
- 2 cobs of corn, halved
- 1 1-pound lobster
- 1 pound crab legs

- 1 pound shrimp
- 1 lemon, cut into wedges

Directions:
1. Set Instant Pot to Sauté mode. Add water, Old Bay, paprika, salt, onion, garlic, thyme, and bay leaves. Bring to a boil. Add potatoes and cook 5 minutes.
2. Stack the remaining ingredients of the lobster bake in this order: chorizo, corn, lobster, crab, shrimp.
3. Close the lid and set the cooking time for 5 minutes on high pressure. Use quick release to remove the steam after cooking.
4. Transfer potatoes, chorizo, corn, lobster, crab, and shrimp to a bowl. Discard bay leaf and thyme sprigs. Serve with lemon.

Nutritional Value Per Serving:
Calories 700
Fat 25.36 g
Carbohydrates 39.55 g
Protein 80.66 g

New Orleans Gumbo

Prep Time: 10 minutes
Cooking Time: 15 minutes
Servings: 4
Ingredients:
- ½ pound bacon
- ¼ cup flour
- 1 tablespoon olive oil
- ½ pound andouille sausage
- 1 onion, chopped
- 1 stalk celery
- 1 red bell pepper, chopped
- 2 cloves garlic, minced
- ½ teaspoon dried thyme
- 1 pound shrimp
- 1 pound okra, sliced
- 1 can whole plum tomatoes
- 1 cup chicken stock
- 2 bay leaves
- ½ teaspoon salt

- ½ teaspoon black pepper
- ¼ cup fresh parsley

Directions:
1. Set Instant Pot to Sauté and add bacon. Cook until most of the fat is rendered. Use a slotted spoon to remove the bacon to a paper towel, leaving the grease in the pan.
2. Add the flour to the pan and stir to combine with the grease. Cook until the flour browns slightly. Remove the roux to a bowl.
3. Wipe out the pot. Add 1 tablespoon olive oil, then add onion, celery, and red pepper. Cook until onion is translucent. Add garlic and thyme and cook until fragrant.
4. Add shrimp and okra and stir until well coated with seasonings. Pour in tomatoes, stock, bay leaves, and salt and pepper.
5. Close lid and set cooking time to 5 minutes. When cooking time ends, use the quick release to remove the steam.
6. Open the lid and set Instant Pot to Sauté. Bring to a boil and add roux, stirring continuously. Cook until liquid thickens.
7. Top with parsley and serve.

Nutritional Value Per Serving:
Calories 842
Fat 43.97 g
Carbohydrates 25.71 g
Protein 91.63 g

Yogurt Fish Patties

Prep Time: 8-10 min.
Cooking Time: 8 min.
Servings: 4

Ingredients:
- 1 small onion, chopped finely
- 3 tablespoons all-purpose flour
- 1 pound fish fillets, finely chopped
- 1/4 cup Greek yogurt, fat-free
- 1 teaspoon baking soda

Directions:
1. In a mixing bowl, thoroughly mix fish, yogurt, onion, flour, and baking soda.
2. Make 6 balls and press them to make patties.
3. Take your Instant Pot and place over dry kitchen surface; open its top lid and switch it on.
4. Press "Sauté". Grease the pot with some cooking oil.
5. Add the patties and cook for 3-4 minutes on each side. Serve warm.

Nutritional Value Per Serving:
Calories 288
Fat 14g
Carbohydrates 30g

Protein 11g

New England Clam Chowder

Prep Time: 10 minutes
Cooking Time: 15 minutes
Servings: 6
Ingredients:
- ½ pound bacon
- 1 onion, chopped
- 1 stalk celery, chopped
- 2 cups clam juice
- 1 pound potatoes, cubed
- 1 bay leaf
- 2 sprigs thyme
- 1 pound clam meat

- 1 cup cream
- ½ teaspoon salt
- ½ teaspoon pepper

Directions:
1. Set the Instant Pot to Saute mode. Add the bacon and cook until most of the fat is rendered. Add onion and celery and cook until onion is translucent.
2. Add clam juice, potatoes, bay leaf, and thyme and enough water to cover.
3. Close the lid and set the cooking time for 5 minutes on high pressure.
4. When steam releases, open the lid and add the clams. Set the pot to Sauté mode and cook 5 minutes or until clams are plump and cooked through. Pour in the cream and stir until heated through.
5. Season to taste with salt and pepper.

Nutritional Value Per Serving:
Calories 467
Fat 30.73 g
Carbohydrates 28.52 g
Protein 19.02 g

Wisconsin Fish Boil

Prep Time: 10 minutes
Cooking Time: 9 minutes
Servings: 4
Ingredients:
- 4 cups water
- 1 pound small red potatoes, halved
- 1 large onion, diced
- 2 carrots, sliced
- 2 stalks celery, sliced
- 1 lemon, halved
- 1 teaspoon salt
- ½ teaspoon pepper
- 2 pounds whitefish

Directions:
1. Place water, potatoes, carrots, onion, lemon, salt, and pepper into the Instant Pot.
2. Close the lid and set the cooking time for 7 minutes. Use quick release to remove the steam.

3. Add the whitefish to the pot. Close the lid and set the cooking time for 2 minutes.
4. Use quick release to remove the steam. Serve with buttered rolls.

Nutritional Value Per Serving:
Calories 405
Fat 13.54 g
Carbohydrates 23.29 g
Protein 46.08 g

Foil-Steamed Tilapia

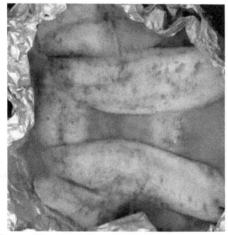

Prep Time: 10 minutes
Cooking Time: 3 minutes
Servings: 2
Ingredients:
- 4 tilapia fillets
- Juice of 1 lemon
- ½ tablespoon olive oil
- ½ teaspoon salt
- ½ teaspoon black pepper

- 4 garlic cloves
- 3 sprigs fresh dill

Directions:
1. Place the fillets on top of a sheet of aluminum foil. Season on both sides with lemon, olive oil, salt, and pepper. Place garlic and dill on top of the fish. Add another sheet of aluminum foil on top and fold in the edges to seal.
2. Pour 2 cups of water into the Instant Pot and add the foil package. Close the lid and set the cooking time for 3 minutes at high pressure.
3. Use quick release to remove the steam.

Nutritional Value Per Serving:
Calories 269
Fat 7.46 g
Carbohydrates 4.14 g
Protein 47.14 g

Mussels Bowls

Prep time: 5 minutes
Cooking time: 7 minutes
Servings: 4

Ingredients:
- 2 pounds mussels, scrubbed
- 12 ounces veggie stock
- 1 tablespoon olive oil
- 1 yellow onion, chopped
- 8 ounces spicy sausage, chopped
- 1 tablespoon sweet paprika

Directions:
1. Set your instant pot on Sauté mode, add oil, heat it up, add onion and sausages, stir and cook for 5 minutes.
2. Add stock, paprika and mussels, stir, cover, cook on Low for 2 minutes, divide into bowls and serve as an appetizer.

Nutritional Value Per Serving:
Calories 112
Fat 4
Carbs 4
Protein 10

Southern Shrimp and Grits

Prep Time: 5 minutes
Cooking Time: 15 minutes
Servings: 6

Ingredients:
- 2 tablespoons butter
- 1 cup grits
- 4 cups chicken stock
- 1 cup shredded Cheddar cheese
- ¼ teaspoon salt
- ½ teaspoon black pepper
- ¼ pound bacon
- 1 shallot, chopped
- 1 garlic clove, minced
- 1 pound shrimp
- Juice of 1 lemon

Directions:

1. Set the Instant Pot to Sauté mode. Melt butter in the pan. Add grits and toast about 30 seconds. Pour stock over grits, add cheese, salt, and pepper, and stir.
2. Close the lid and set cooking time to 10 minutes. After cooking time, use the quick release to remove steam. Pour grits into a bowl and cover to keep warm.
3. Wipe out the pot. Set to Sauté and add bacon and cook until most of the fat renders. Add shallot and garlic cook until shallot is translucent. Add shrimp and cook through about 3 minutes. Squeeze lemon juice over shrimp. Pour contents of pot over grits.

Nutritional Value Per Serving:
Calories 1006
Fat 37.32 g
Carbohydrates 7.09 g
Protein 152.5 g

Swordfish Fra Diavolo

Prep Time: 10 minutes
Cooking Time: 5 minutes
Servings: 2

Ingredients:
- 2 tablespoons olive oil
- 4 garlic cloves, minced
- ½ teaspoon red pepper flakes
- 1 can whole peeled tomatoes, crushed
- ½ teaspoon salt
- ½ teaspoon black pepper
- 1 pound swordfish steaks

Directions:
1. Set the Instant Pot to sauté mode. Add garlic and red pepper flakes and cook until fragrant. Add tomatoes, salt, and pepper.
2. Place swordfish in the sauce. Flip once to coat.
3. Close lid and set cooking time to 3 minutes. After cooking time, use the quick release to remove steam. Serve with pasta.

Nutritional Value Per Serving:
Calories 427
Fat 28.88 g
Carbohydrates 5.81 g
Protein 45.81 g

Cajun Crab Etouffee

Prep Time: 10 minutes
Cooking Time: 35 minutes
Servings: 4
Ingredients:
- 1 cup uncooked white rice
- ¼ cups water
- ¼ cup butter
- ¼ cup flour
- 1 tablespoon olive oil
- 1 onion, chopped
- 1 celery stalk, chopped
- 1 bell pepper, chopped
- garlic cloves, minced
- 1 teaspoon Creole seasoning
- ½ cup white wine
- 1 cup chicken stock

- 1 tablespoon tomato paste
- cups fresh cooked crabmeat
- ¼ cup fresh parsley, chopped

Directions:
1. Combine water and rice in the pot. Close lid and cook on Rice Cooker mode. Transfer rice to a covered dish and set aside. Wipe out the pot.
2. Set Instant Pot to Sauté mode and melt butter in the pot. Add flour and cook until roux is brown. Transfer to a bowl. Wipe out the pot.
3. Add olive oil to the pan, followed by onion, celery, bell pepper, garlic, and Creole seasoning. Cook until onion is translucent, then deglaze the pan with white wine.
4. Add chicken stock, tomato paste, and crabmeat. Bring to a boil. Add roux and cook, stirring constantly, until thickened. Close lid and set cooking time for 5 minutes on high pressure.
5. Serve etouffee over rice. Top with fresh parsley.

Nutritional Value Per Serving:
Calories 709
Fat 22.28 g
Carbohydrates 51.99 g
Protein 65.72 g

Chinese Takeout Shrimp Fried Rice

Prep Time: 10 minutes
Cooking Time: 35 minutes
Servings: 4
Ingredients:
- 1 cup white rice
- ¼ cup water
- 1 pound shrimp
- 1 cup water
- tablespoons olive oil
- 1 egg, beaten
- garlic cloves, minced
- 2 tablespoons soy sauce
- ¼ cup green onions, sliced

Directions:
1. Combine rice and 1 ¼ cups water in the Instant Pot. Cook on Rice Cooker mode. Transfer to a bowl and set aside. Wipe out the pot.
2. Pour the water into the Instant Pot and place a steamer basket over the water. Arrange shrimp in the basket. Close lid and set cooking time for 1 minute on high pressure.

3. After cooking time, use the quick release to remove the steam. Transfer shrimp to a bowl of cold water. When cool enough to handle, peel and chop the shrimp. Wipe out the pot.
4. Set the Instant Pot to Sauté and add oil. Pour the egg into the pan and scramble into small grains.
5. Add garlic and cook until fragrant. Pour in rice, chopped shrimp, and soy sauce and toss until well combined. Serve.

Nutritional Value Per Serving:
Calories 355
Fat 8.73 g
Carbohydrates 39.9 g
Protein 28.19 g

Spicy Mussels

Prep time: 10 minutes
Cooking time: 6 minutes
Servings: 4
Ingredients:
- 2 pounds mussels, scrubbed
- 2 tablespoons olive oil
- 1 yellow onion, chopped
- ½ cup chicken stock
- ½ teaspoon red pepper flakes
- 14 ounces tomatoes, chopped
- 2 teaspoons garlic, minced
- 2 teaspoons oregano, dried

Directions:
1. Set your instant pot on Sauté mode, add oil, heat it up, add onions, stir and sauté for 3 minutes.
2. Add pepper flakes, garlic, stock, tomatoes, oregano and mussels, stir, cover and cook on Low for 3 minutes.
3. Divide mussels into small bowls and serve as an appetizer.

Nutritional Value Per Serving:
Calories 82
Fat 1g

Carbs 3g
Protein 2g

Chapter 4: Poultry Recipes

Mustard Lemon Turkey

Prep Time: 5 min
Cooking Time: 15 min
Servings: 3

Ingredients:
- 1 pound turkey thigh, boneless
- 1 tablespoon oil
- ½ cup chicken broth
- 1 tablespoon Italian seasoning
- tablespoons lemon juice
- 2 tablespoons Dijon mustard
- Salt and pepper, to taste

Directions:
1. Dust the turkey with salt and pepper.
2. Put oil and dusted turkey in the 3-quart Instant Pot Mini.
3. Combine the Dijon mustard with chicken broth, Italian seasoning, and lemon juice in a bowl.
4. Pour the Dijon mustard mixture over the turkey in the Instant Pot Mini.
5. Fasten the lid and cook on high pressure for 15 minutes.

6. Once the Instant Pot Mini comes to pressure, then the selected cook time will begin.
7. Naturally release the pressure and shift the contents of the pot to a bowl.
8. Serve hot.

Nutritional Value Per Serving:
Calories: 225
Fat: 9.1g
Carbohydrates: 1.6g
Protein: 32.1g

Teriyaki Chicken Thighs

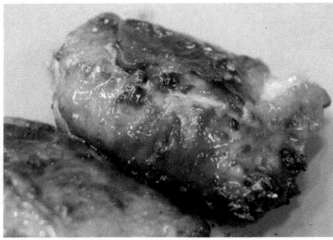

Prep Time: 10 min
Cooking Time: 10 min
Servings: 2

Ingredients:
- 2 tablespoons brown sugar, packed
- 2 tablespoons soy sauce
- 1½ tablespoons rice wine vinegar
- 1 teaspoon fresh ginger, finely grated
- 1¼ pounds chicken thighs, boneless, skinless, chunked

- ¾ tablespoon avocado oil
- ¾ teaspoon garlic, minced
- 1½ teaspoons sesame oil
- ¾ tablespoon cornstarch

Directions:
1. For teriyaki sauce: Combine the brown sugar with soy sauce, rice wine vinegar, sesame oil, garlic, and ginger in a bowl.
2. Put oil, chicken and teriyaki sauce in the 3-quart Instant Pot Mini.
3. Fasten the lid and cook on high pressure for 5 minutes.
4. Once the Instant Pot Mini comes to pressure, then the selected cook time will begin.
5. Naturally release the pressure and keep the Instant Pot Mini warm.
6. Stir cornstarch with 1 tablespoon of water and whisk it in the chicken teriyaki.
7. Press "Sauté" and sauté for about 5 minutes.
8. Shift the contents of the pot to a bowl and serve hot.

Nutritional Value Per Serving:
Calories: 517
Fat: 25g
Carbohydrates: 24g
Protein: 51g

Coconut Turmeric Chicken

Prep time: 2 minutes
Cooking Time: 15 minutes
Servings: 4
Ingredients:
- 2 pounds of skinless, boneless chicken thighs
- 1 can of coconut cream
- 1 tablespoon of turmeric

Directions:
1. Place the thighs in the Instant Pot, add the coconut cream and turmeric. Gently mix everything together until it's combined.
2. Choose the poultry setting on your cooker, set the pressure to high and the timer to 15 minutes.
3. Release the pressure quickly after that time, taste for seasoning (add salt and pepper as needed) and serve alongside your preferred side dishes!

Nutritional Value Per Serving:
Calories: 321
Fat: 11.8 g
Carbs: 8.8 g
Proteins: 45 g

Noodle Chicken Soup

Prep Time: 15 min
Cooking Time: 20 min
Servings: 4

Ingredients:
- ¼ onion, diced
- 1 celery stalk, sliced
- ¼ teaspoon salt
- 1/8 teaspoon ground turmeric
- 1½ cups chicken broth, low-salt
- ½ tablespoon butter, unsalted
- ½ dried bay leaf
- 1 carrot, sliced
- ¼ teaspoon black pepper
- ½ chicken breast, boneless and skinless
- ½ cup egg noodles
- Fresh parsley, for garnish

Directions:
1. Put butter and onions in the 3-quart Instant Pot Mini and press "Sauté".
2. Sauté for about 5 minutes and stir in the remaining ingredients except noodles and parsley.
3. Fasten the lid and cook on high pressure for 15 minutes.

4. Once the Instant Pot Mini comes to pressure, then the selected cook time will begin.
5. Naturally release the pressure and remove the chicken.
6. Shred the chicken with fork and return to the Instant Pot Mini along with the noodles.
7. Press "Sauté" and sauté for about 5 minutes, stirring occasionally.
8. Decant the soup in a serving bowl and garnish with parsley to serve.

Nutritional Value Per Serving:
Calories: 81
Fat: 2.8g
Carbohydrates: 7.8g
Protein: 6g

Chicken Liver Curry

Prep time: 15 minutes
Cooking Time: 35 minutes
Servings: 2
Ingredients:
- 1lb diced chicken breast
- 0.5lb diced chicken liver
- 1lb chopped vegetables
- 1 cup broth
- 3tbsp curry paste

Directions:
1. Mix all the ingredients in your Instant Pot.
2. Cook on Stew for 35 minutes.
3. Release the pressure naturally.

Nutritional Value Per Serving:
Calories: 350
Carbs: 10
Fat: 17
Protein: 52

Balsamic Turkey Breast

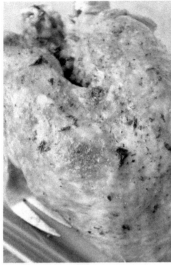

Prep time: 15 minutes
Cooking Time: 35 minutes
Servings: 2

Ingredients:
- 1lb diced turkey breast
- 1lb chopped vegetables
- 1 cup chicken soup
- 2tbsp balsamic reduction

Directions:
1. Mix all the ingredients in your Instant Pot.
2. Cook on Stew for 35 minutes.
3. Release the pressure naturally.

Nutritional Value Per Serving:
Calories: 295
Carbs: 5
Fat: 14
Protein: 46

Mediterranean Turkey Cutlets

Prep Time: 10 min
Cooking Time: 8 min
Servings: 3

Ingredients:
- 1 teaspoon Greek seasoning
- 1 pound turkey cutlets
- 2 tablespoons olive oil
- 1 teaspoon turmeric powder
- ½ cup all-purpose flour
- Tomato sauce, for serving

Directions:
1. Combine the turkey cutlets with all-purpose flour, Greek seasoning, and turmeric powder in a bowl.
2. Put oil and turkey cutlets in the 3-quart Instant Pot Mini.
3. Fasten the lid and cook on high pressure for 8 minutes.
4. Once the Instant Pot Mini comes to pressure, then the selected cook time will begin.
5. Naturally release the pressure and shift the contents of the pot to a platter.
6. Serve immediately.

Nutritional Value Per Serving:
Calories: 321

Fat: 10.2g
Carbohydrates: 16.9g
Protein: 39.8g

Tex Max Chicken

Prep Time: 5 min
Cooking Time: 12 min
Servings: 3
Ingredients:
- ½ cup tomato sauce
- 1 pound chicken breasts
- ¼ cup salsa
- ½ cup tomatoes, diced
- 1 tablespoon Mexican seasoning
- ¼ teaspoon salt
- ½ cup green chilies

Directions:

1. Put the chicken breasts along with the remaining ingredients in the 3-quart Instant Pot Mini.
2. Fasten the lid and cook on high pressure for 12 minutes.
3. Once the Instant Pot Mini comes to pressure, then the selected cook time will begin.
4. Naturally release the pressure and shift the contents of the pot to a platter.
5. Serve hot.

Nutritional Value Per Serving:
Calories: 336
Fat: 11.7g
Carbohydrates: 10.5g
Protein: 45.8g

Whole Chicken Chili

Prep Time: 5 min
Cooking Time: 30 min
Servings: 3

Ingredients:
- ¾ cup homemade chicken broth
- ½ tablespoon cayenne pepper
- 1 pound whole chicken, neck and giblet removed
- ¾ tablespoon olive oil
- 2 small green chilies, chopped
- Salt and black pepper, to taste

Directions:
1. Dust the chicken with cayenne pepper, salt, and black pepper.
2. Put the oil and chicken in the 3-quart Instant Pot Mini.
3. Press "SAUTÉ" and sauté for about 6 minutes.
4. Remove the chicken from the Instant Pot Mini and arrange a trivet in it.
5. Put the chicken on the trivet and add the broth.
6. Fasten the lid and cook on high pressure for 24 minutes.
7. Once the Instant Pot Mini comes to pressure, then the selected cook time will begin.
8. Naturally release the pressure and shift the chicken to a platter.

9   Top with green chilies and serve hot.

Nutritional Value Per Serving:
Calories: 330
Fat: 15.2g
Carbohydrates: 0.9g
Protein: 45.1g

Salsa Chicken Steak

Prep Time: 5 min
Cooking Time: 8 hours
Servings: 3
Ingredients:
- ½ cup tomato sauce
- ¼ teaspoon garlic powder
- 1 pound chicken steak
- 1 cup salsa
- ¼ cup shredded Monterey Jack cheese
- ¼ teaspoon hot pepper sauce
- Salt and pepper, to taste

Directions:
1. Dust the chicken steak with garlic powder, salt, and black pepper.
2. Combine salsa with tomato sauce and hot pepper in a bowl.
3. Place a steamer basket in the 3-quart Instant Pot Mini and arrange steak pieces on it.
4. Top with the salsa mixture and fasten the lid.
5. Select "slow cooker" and "Medium" for 8 hours.
6. Naturally release the pressure and shift the chicken to a platter to serve.

Nutritional Value Per Serving:

Calories: 350
Fat: 20.5g
Carbohydrates: 7.9g
Protein: 32.3g

Turkey And Parsnips Curry

Prep time: 15 minutes
Cooking Time: 20 minutes
Servings: 2
Ingredients:
- 0.5lb parsnip
- 0.5lb chopped cooked turkey
- 1 thinly sliced onion
- 1 cup curry sauce
- 1tbsp oil or ghee

Directions:
1. Set the Instant Pot to saute and add the onion and oil.
2. When the onion is soft, add the remaining ingredients and seal.
3. Cook on Stew for 20 minutes.
4. Release the pressure naturally.

Nutritional Value Per Serving:
Calories: 400

Carbs: 27
Fat: 15
Protein: 43

Turkey Dinner Casserole

Prep time: 15 minutes
Cooking Time: 10 minutes
Servings: 2
Ingredients:
- 1lb cooked shredded turkey
- 1lb chopped vegetables
- 1 cup low sugar honey mustard sauce
- 1tbsp mixed herbs
- 1 minced onion

Directions:
1. Mix all the ingredients in your Instant Pot.
2. Cook on Stew for 10 minutes. Release the pressure naturally.

Nutritional Value Per Serving:
Calories: 400
Carbs: 34
Fat: 13
Protein: 39

Pulled Chicken

Prep time: 15 minutes
Cooking Time: 35 minutes
Servings: 2

Ingredients:
- 1.5lb chicken breast
- shredded onions
- 1 cup low sodium broth
- 1 cup BBQ sauce

Directions:
1. Mix all the ingredients in your Instant Pot.
2. Cook on Stew for 35 minutes.
3. Release the pressure naturally.
4. Shred the chicken.

Nutritional Value Per Serving:
Calories: 290
Carbs: 7
Fat: 7
Protein: 45

Half Roast Chicken

Prep time: 15 minutes
Cooking Time: 35 minutes
Servings: 2

Ingredients:
- Half a chicken
- 2tbsp mixed herbs
- 2tbsp rub
- 1 cup low sodium broth

Directions:
1. Mix all the herbs, rub, and a little broth and rub it into the chicken.
2. Pour the broth in your Instant Pot and lower the chicken, bones down.
3. Cook on Stew for 35 minutes.
4. Release the pressure naturally.

Nutritional Value Per Serving:
Calories: 300
Carbs: 6
Fat: 9
Protein: 43

Turkey Zoodles

Prep time: 15 minutes
Cooking Time: 35 minutes
Servings: 2
Ingredients:
- 1lb diced turkey
- 1lb spiralized zucchini
- 1 cup diced vegetables
- 1 cup low sodium chicken broth

Directions:
1. Mix all the ingredients except the zucchini in your Instant Pot.
2. Cook on Stew for 35 minutes.
3. Release the pressure naturally.
4. Stir in the zucchini and allow to warm through before serving.

Nutritional Value Per Serving:
Calories: 250
Carbs: 4
Fat: 7
Protein: 39

Chicken Coconut Curry

Prep time: 15 minutes
Cooking Time: 20 minutes
Servings: 2
Ingredients:
- 0.5lb chopped cooked chicken breast
- 1 thinly sliced onion
- 1 cup coconut milk
- 3tbsp curry paste
- 1tbsp oil or ghee

Directions:
1. Set the Instant Pot to saute and add the onion, oil, and curry paste.
2. When the onion is soft, add the remaining ingredients and seal.
3. Cook on Stew for 20 minutes.
4. Release the pressure naturally.

Nutritional Value Per Serving:
Calories: 450
Carbs: 27
Fat: 25
Protein: 43

Turkey Meatball Stew

Prep time: 15 minutes
Cooking Time: 35 minutes
Servings: 2
Ingredients:
- 1lb minced turkey
- 1lb chopped vegetables
- 1 cup chicken soup
- 3tbsp almond flour
- 2tbsp mixed seasoning

Directions:
1. Roll the turkey into meatballs with the seasoning and almond flour.
2. Mix all the ingredients in your Instant Pot.
3. Cook on Stew for 35 minutes.
4. Release the pressure naturally.

Nutritional Value Per Serving:
Calories: 260
Carbs: 6
Fat: 7
Protein: 38

Duck And Bean Stew

Prep time: 15 minutes
Cooking Time: 35 minutes
Servings: 2

Ingredients:
- 1lb diced duck breast
- 1lb cooked black beans
- 1 cup low sodium vegetable broth
- 1tbsp 5 spice seasoning

Directions:
1. Mix all the ingredients in your Instant Pot.
2. Cook on Stew for 35 minutes.
3. Release the pressure naturally.

Nutritional Value Per Serving:
Calories: 360
Carbs: 16
Fat: 14
Protein: 39

Chicken Zoodle Soup

Prep time: 15 minutes
Cooking Time: 35 minutes
Servings: 2

Ingredients:
- 1lb chopped cooked chicken
- 1lb spiralized zucchini
- 1 cup low sodium chicken soup
- 1 cup diced vegetables

Directions:
1. Mix all the ingredients except the zucchini in your Instant Pot.
2. Cook on Stew for 35 minutes.
3. Release the pressure naturally.
4. Stir in the zucchini and allow to heat thoroughly.

Nutritional Value Per Serving:
Calories: 250
Carbs: 5
Fat: 10
Protein: 40

Turkey And Spaghetti Squash

Prep time: 15 minutes
Cooking Time: 35 minutes
Servings: 2
Ingredients:
- 1lb minced turkey
- 1 cup chicken broth
- 1tbsp mixed Italian herbs
- ½ spaghetti squash, to fit the Instant Pot

Directions:
1. Mix the herbs into the turkey.
2. Pack the turkey into the squash.
3. Pour the broth in your Instant Pot.
4. Put the squash into the Instant Pot.
5. Cook on Stew for 35 minutes.
6. Release the pressure naturally.
7. Shred the squash and mix the "spaghetti" with the turkey.

Nutritional Value Per Serving:
Calories: 260
Carbs: 5
Fat: 5
Protein: 41

Chapter 5: Vegan Recipes

Barley with Vegetables

Prep time: 10 minutes
Cooking time: 25 minutes
Servings: 4
Ingredients:
- 1 tablespoon extra-virgin olive oil
- 1 tablespoon butter
- 1 white onion, peeled and chopped
- 1 garlic clove, peeled and minced
- 1½ cups pearl barley, rinsed
- 1 celery stalk, chopped
- ⅓ cup mushrooms, chopped
- cups vegetable stock
- 2¼ cups water

- Salt and ground black pepper, to taste
- tablespoons fresh parsley, chopped

Directions:
1. Set the Instant Pot on Sauté mode, add the oil and butter and heat them up.
2. Add the onion and garlic, stir, and cook for 4 minutes. Add the celery and barley and toss to coat.
3. Add the mushrooms, water, stock, salt, and pepper, stir, cover the Instant Pot and cook on the Multigrain setting for 18 minutes.
4. Release the pressure, uncover the Instant Pot, add the cheese and parsley and more salt and pepper, if needed, stir for 2 minutes, divide into bowls, and serve.

Nutritional Value Per Serving:
Calories: 170
Fat: 6
Carbs: 30
Protein: 8

Cracked Wheat and Vegetables

Prep time: 10 minutes
Cooking time: 15 minutes
Servings: 4
Ingredients:
- ½ cup cracked whole wheat
- 1½ cups water
- tomatoes, cored and chopped
- 2 small potatoes, cubed
- cauliflower florets, chopped
- Salt and ground black pepper, to taste
- ¼ teaspoon mustard seeds
- ¼ teaspoon cumin seeds
- 1 teaspoon ginger, grated
- 1 tablespoon yellow split peas, rinsed
- 2 garlic cloves, peeled and minced
- 1 yellow onion, peeled and chopped
- 2 curry leaves
- teaspoons vegetable oil
- ¼ teaspoon garam masala

- Cilantro leaves, chopped, for serving

Directions:
1. Set the Instant Pot on Sauté mode, add the oil and heat it up.
2. Add the cumin and mustard seeds, stir, and cook for 1 minute.
3. Add the onion, garlic, split peas, garam masala, ginger, and curry leaves, stir, and cook for 2 minutes.
4. Add the cauliflower, potatoes, and tomatoes, stir, and cook for 4 minutes.
5. Add the wheat, salt, pepper, and water, stir, cover, and cook on Multigrain mode for 5 minutes.
6. Release the pressure, uncover the Instant Pot, transfer the wheat and vegetables to plates, sprinkle cilantro on top, and serve.

Nutritional Value Per Serving:
Calories: 145
Fat: 2
Carbs: 16
Protein: 7

Cracked Wheat Surprise

Prep time: 5 minutes
Cooking time: 17 minutes
Servings: 2
Ingredients:
- cups cracked wheat
- 1 teaspoon fennel seeds
- 2½ cups butter
- 2 cups light brown sugar
- cloves
- 1 cup almond milk
- Salt
- cups water
- Almonds, chopped

Directions:
1. Set the Instant Pot on Sauté mode, add the butter and heat it up. Add the cracked wheat, stir, and cook for 5 minutes.
2. Add the cloves and fennel seeds, stir, and cook for 2 minutes. Add the sugar, a pinch of salt, almond milk, and water, stir, cover, and cook on the Multigrain setting for 10 minutes.
3. Release the pressure, uncover the Instant Pot, divide into bowls, and serve with chopped almonds on top.

Nutritional Value Per Serving:

Calories: 120
Fat: 1
Carbs: 4
Protein: 8

Barley Salad

Prep time: 10 minutes
Cooking time: 20 minutes
Servings: 4
Ingredients:
- 1 cup hulled barley, rinsed
- 2½ cups water
- ¾ cup jarred spinach pesto
- 1 green apple, chopped
- ¼ cup celery, chopped
- Salt and ground white pepper, to taste

Directions:
1. Put the barley, water, salt, and pepper into the Instant Pot, stir, cover and cook on the Multigrain setting for 20 minutes.

2. Release the pressure, uncover the Instant Pot, strain the barley, and put in a bowl.
3. Add the celery, apple, spinach pesto, and more salt and pepper, toss to coat, and serve.

Nutritional Value Per Serving:
Calories: 170
Fat: 7
Carbs: 0
Protein: 5

Wheat Berry Salad

Prep time: 10 minutes
Cooking time: 35 minutes
Servings: 6
Ingredients:
- 1½ cups wheat berries
- 1 tablespoon extra-virgin olive oil
- Salt and ground black pepper, to taste
- cups water

For the salad:
- 1 tablespoon balsamic vinegar
- 1 tablespoon extra-virgin olive oil
- 1 cup cherry tomatoes, cut into halves
- green onions, chopped
- ½ cup Kalamata olives, pitted and chopped
- ½ cup fresh basil leaves, chopped
- ½ cup fresh parsley, chopped

Directions:
1. Set the Instant Pot on Sauté mode, add the tablespoon oil and heat it up.
2. Add the wheat berries, stir, and cook for 5 minutes. Add the water, salt, and pepper, cover the Instant Pot, and cook on Multigrain mode for 30 minutes.

3. Release the pressure for 10 minutes, uncover the Instant Pot, drain the wheat berries, and put them in a salad bowl.
4. Add the salt and pepper, 1 tablespoon oil, balsamic vinegar, tomatoes, green onions, olives, basil, and parsley, toss to coat, and serve.

Nutritional Value Per Serving:
Calories: 240
Fat: 11
Carbs: 31
Protein: 5

Bulgur Salad

Prep time: 15 minutes
Cooking time: 12 minutes
Servings: 4

Ingredients:
- Zest from 1 orange
- Juice from 2 oranges
- garlic cloves, minced
- 2 teaspoons canola oil
- 2 tablespoons ginger, grated
- 1 cup bulgur, rinsed
- 1 tablespoon soy sauce
- ⅔ cup scallions, chopped
- ⅓ cup almonds, chopped
- Salt, to taste
- 2 teaspoons brown sugar
- ½ cups water

Directions:
1. Set the Instant Pot on Sauté mode, add the oil and heat it up. Add the ginger and garlic, stir, and cook for 1 minutes.
2. Add the bulgur, sugar, water, and orange juice, stir, cover, and cook on the Multigrain setting for 5 minutes.

3. Release the pressure naturally, uncover the Instant Pot, and set the bulgur aside. Heat up a pan over medium heat, add the almonds, stir, and toast them for 3 minutes.
4. Add the orange zest, salt, soy sauce and scallions, stir, and cook for 1 minute. Add this to bulgur mix, stir with a fork, transfer to a bowl, and serve.

Nutritional Value Per Serving:
Calories: 232
Fat: 7
Carbs: 38
Protein: 7

Bulgur Pilaf

Prep time: 10 minutes
Cooking time: 21 minutes
Servings: 6
Ingredients:
- cups red onions, peeled and chopped
- 2 tablespoons extra virgin olive oil
- Salt and ground black pepper, to taste
- 2 teaspoons ginger, grated
- ¼ cup dill, chopped
- 1 garlic clove, peeled and minced
- 1½ cups bulgur
- ¼ cup fresh mint, chopped
- ¼ cup fresh parsley, chopped
- tablespoons lemon juice
- ½ teaspoon cumin
- ½ teaspoons turmeric
- 2 cups vegetable stock
- 1½ cups carrot, chopped
- ½ cup walnuts, toasted and chopped

Directions:

1. Set the Instant Pot on Sauté mode, add the oil and heat it up. Add the onion, stir, and cook on Multigrain temperature for 12 minutes. Add the garlic, stir, and cook for 1 minute.
2. Add the cumin, turmeric, and bulgur, stir, and cook for 1 minute. Add the ginger, stock, carrots, salt, and pepper, stir, cover and cook on the Manual setting for 5 minutes.
3. Release the pressure, uncover the Instant Pot, add the mint, dill, parsley, lemon juice, and more salt and pepper, if needed, and stir gently.
4. Divide among plates, and serve with almonds on top.

Nutritional Value Per Serving:
Calories: 270
Fat: 12
Carbs: 38
Protein: 7

Dill Herbed Carrots

Prep Time: 5 minutes
Cooking Time: 15 minutes
Servings: 4

Ingredients:
- 1 pound whole young carrots, peeled
- 1 cup water
- tablespoons olive oil
- ¼ teaspoon salt
- ¼ teaspoon black pepper
- ¼ cup fresh dill, minced

Directions:
1. Pour water into Instant Pot. Place steamer basket over the water and arrange carrots in the basket. Close the lid and set cooking time for 15 minutes.
2. When carrots are cooked, toss with olive oil, salt, pepper, and dill. Serve warm.

Nutritional Value Per Serving:
Calories 100
Fat 6.97 g
Carbohydrates 9.47 g
Protein 0.9 g

Artichokes with Lemon Butter

Prep Time: 5 minutes
Cooking Time: 10 minutes
Servings: 4
Ingredients:
- whole artichokes, trimmed
- 1 cup water
- ½ cup almond milk, melted
- Juice of 1 lemon
- ¼ teaspoon salt
- ¼ teaspoon black pepper

Directions:
1. Pour water into Instant Pot and place a steamer basket over the water. Arrange artichokes in the steamer basket and close lid. Set cooking time for 10 minutes at high pressure.
2. Meanwhile, whisk together almond milk, lemon juice, salt, and pepper.
3. To eat, remove leaves from artichokes one by one and dip into butter. Use your teeth to scrape off the soft inner layer of the leaves.

Nutritional Value Per Serving:
Calories 245
Fat 23.17 g
Carbohydrates 9.47 g
Protein 2.95 g

Scalloped Potatoes

Prep Time: 20 minutes
Cooking Time: 50 minutes
Servings: 6

Ingredients:
- large potatoes, peeled and sliced into ¼ inch thick rounds
- cups almond milk
- ¼ cup vegan butter
- ¼ cup flour
- 1 cup + ¼ cup grated vegan cheese
- ¼ teaspoon salt
- ¼ teaspoon black pepper

Directions:
1. Set the Instant Pot to Saute and add vegan butter. When butter is melted, stir in flour. Cook until bubbling subsides and mixture has darkened slightly.
2. Pour in almond milk, stirring constantly, and cook until thickened. Add 1 cup vegan cheese and stir until melted. Turn off heat.

3. Arrange a layer of potato slices on the bottom of a baking dish that fits into the Instant Pot. Top with a layer of cheese sauce, followed by another layer of potato slices. Continue this sequence until all the sauce and potatoes are used up. Sprinkle with remaining cheese. Wash out the inner pot.
4. Place trivet in the pot and add enough water to reach the top of the trivet. Place baking dish over trivet. Close lid and set cooking time to 35 minutes on high pressure.
5. If desired, place casserole under the broiler for 2-5 minutes to the brown top after cooking is complete.

Nutritional Value Per Serving:
Calories 375
Fat 18.56 g
Carbohydrates 40.58 g
Protein 12.61 g

Chapter 6: Soup & Stew Recipes

Cheese and Potato Soup

Prep time: 10 minutes
Cooking time: 10 minutes
Servings: 6
Ingredients:
- cups potatoes, cubed
- tablespoons butter
- ½ cup yellow onion, chopped
- 28 ounces chicken stock
- Salt and ground black pepper, to taste
- tablespoons dried parsley
- 1/8 teaspoon red pepper flakes
- 2 tablespoons cornstarch
- 2 tablespoons water
- ounces cream cheese, cubed
- 2 cups half and half

- 1 cup cheddar cheese, shredded
- 1 cup corn
- bacon slices, cooked and crumbled

Directions:
1. Set the Instant Pot on Sauté mode, add the butter and melt it. Add the onion, stir, and cook 5 minutes.
2. Add half of the stock, salt, pepper, pepper flakes, and parsley and stir. Put the potatoes in the steamer basket, cover the Instant Pot and cook on the Steam setting for 4 minutes.
3. Release the pressure fast, uncover the Instant Pot, and transfer the potatoes to a bowl.
4. In another bowl, mix the cornstarch with water and stir well. Set the Instant Pot to Manual mode, add the cornstarch slurry, cream cheese, and shredded cheese and stir well. Add the rest of the stock, corn, bacon, potatoes, half and half. Stir, bring to a simmer, ladle into bowls, and serve.

Nutritional Value Per Serving:
Calories: 188
Fat: 7.14
Fiber: 1.5
Carbs: 22
Protein: 9

Mushroom Tofu Stew

Prep time: 15 minutes
Cooking Time: 10 minutes
Servings: 2
Ingredients:
- 1lb chopped mushrooms
- 1lb chopped tofu
- 1 cup mushroom soup
- 1tbsp mixed herbs
- 1 minced onion

Directions:
1. Mix all the ingredients in your Instant Pot.
2. Cook on Stew for 10 minutes.
3. Release the pressure naturally.

Nutritional Value Per Serving:
Calories: 180
Carbs: 5
Fat: 11
Protein: 34

Split Pea Soup

Prep time: 10 minutes
Cooking time: 20 minutes
Servings: 6

Ingredients:
- tablespoons butter
- 1 pound chicken sausage, ground
- 1 yellow onion, peeled and chopped
- ½ cup carrots, peeled and chopped
- ½ cup celery, chopped
- garlic cloves, peeled and minced
- 29 ounces chicken stock
- Salt and ground black pepper, to taste
- 2 cups water
- 16 ounces split peas, rinsed
- ½ cup half and half
- ¼ teaspoon red pepper flakes

Directions:
1. Set the Instant Pot on Sauté mode, add the sausage, brown it on all sides and transfer to a plate. Add the butter to the Instant Pot and melt it.

2. Add the celery, onions, and carrots, stir, and cook 4 minutes. Add the garlic, stir and cook for 1 minute. Add the water, stock, peas and pepper flakes, stir, cover and cook on the Soup setting for 10 minutes.
3. Release the pressure, puree the mix using an immersion blender and set the Instant Pot on Manual mode.
4. Add the sausage, salt, pepper, and half and half, stir, bring to a simmer, and ladle into soup bowls.

Nutritional Value Per Serving:
Calories: 30
Fat: 11
Carbs: 14
Protein: 20

Corn Soup

Prep time: 10 minutes
Cooking time: 15 minutes
Servings: 4
Ingredients:
- leeks, chopped
- tablespoons butter
- 2 garlic cloves, peeled and minced
- ears of corn, kernels cut off, cobs reserved
- 2 bay leaves
- tarragon sprigs, chopped
- 1-quart chicken stock
- Salt and ground black pepper, to taste
- Extra virgin olive oil
- 1 tablespoon fresh chives, chopped

Directions:
1. Set the Instant Pot on Sauté mode, add the butter and melt it. Add the garlic and leeks, stir, and cook for 4 minutes.
2. Add the corn, corn cobs, bay leaves, tarragon, and stock to cover everything, cover the Instant Pot and cook on the Soup setting for 15 minutes.
3. Release the pressure, uncover the Instant Pot, discard the bay leaves and corn cobs, and transfer everything to a blender.

4. Pulse well to obtain a smooth soup, add the rest of the stock and blend again.
5. Add the salt and pepper, stir well, divide into soup bowls, and serve cold with chives and olive oil on top.

Nutritional Value Per Serving:
Calories: 300
Fat: 8.3
Carbs: 50
Protein: 13

Chicken Noodle Soup

Prep time: 10 minutes
Cooking time: 12 minutes
Servings: 6
Ingredients:
- 1 yellow onion, peeled and chopped
- 1 tablespoon butter
- 1 celery stalk, chopped

- carrots, peeled and sliced
- Salt and ground black pepper, to taste
- cups chicken stock
- cups chicken, already cooked and shredded
- Egg noodles, already cooked

Directions:
1. Set the Instant Pot on Sauté mode, add the butter and heat it up. Add the onion, stir, and cook 2 minutes.
2. Add the celery and carrots, stir, and cook 5 minutes. Add the chicken and stock, stir, cover the Instant Pot and cook on the Soup setting for 5 minutes.
3. Release the pressure, uncover the Instant Pot, add salt and pepper to taste, and stir. Divide the noodles into soup bowls, add the soup over them, and serve.

Nutritional Value Per Serving:
Calories: 100
Fat: 1
Carbs: 4
Protein: 7

Zuppa Toscana

Prep time: 10 minutes
Cooking time: 17 minutes
Servings: 8
Ingredients:
- 1 pound chicken sausage, ground
- bacon slices, chopped
- garlic cloves, peeled and minced
- 1 cup yellow onion, peeled and chopped
- 1 tablespoon butter
- 40 ounces chicken stock
- Salt and ground black pepper, to taste
- Red pepper flakes
- potatoes, cubed
- tablespoons cornstarch
- 12 ounces evaporated milk
- 1 cup Parmesan, shredded
- cup spinach, chopped

Directions:

1. Set the Instant Pot on Sauté mode, add the bacon, stir, cook until it's crispy, and transfer to a plate.
2. Add the sausage to the Instant Pot, stir, cook until it browns on all sides, and also transfer to a plate.
3. Add the butter to the Instant Pot and melt it. Add the onion, stir, and cook for 5 minutes. Add the garlic, stir, and cook for 1 minute. Add ⅓ of the stock, salt, pepper, and pepper flakes and stir.
4. Place the potatoes in the steamer basket of the Instant Pot, cover and cook on the Steam setting for 4 minutes.
5. Release the pressure, uncover the Instant Pot, and transfer the potatoes to a bowl. Add the rest of the stock to the Instant Pot with the cornstarch mixed with the evaporated milk, stir, and set the Instant Pot on Manual mode.
6. Add the cheese, sausage, bacon, potatoes, spinach, more salt and pepper, if needed, stir, divide into bowls, and serve.

Nutritional Value Per Serving:
Calories: 170
Fat: 4
Carbs: 24
Protein: 10

Minestrone Soup

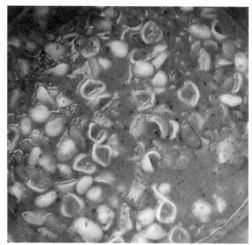

Prep time: 10 minutes
Cooking time: 15 minutes
Servings: 8
Ingredients:
- 1 tablespoon extra-virgin olive oil
- 1 celery stalk, chopped
- carrots, peeled and chopped
- 1 onion, peeled and chopped
- 1 cup corn kernels
- 1 zucchini, chopped
- pounds tomatoes, cored, peeled, and chopped
- garlic cloves, peeled and minced
- 29 ounces chicken stock
- 1 cup uncooked pasta
- Salt and ground black pepper, to taste
- 1 teaspoon Italian seasoning
- cups baby spinach
- 15 ounces canned kidney beans
- 1 cup Asiago cheese, grated

- 2 tablespoons fresh basil, chopped

Directions:
1. Set the Instant Pot on Sauté mode, add the oil and heat it up. Add the onion, stir, and cook for 5 minutes.
2. Add the carrots, garlic, celery, corn, and zucchini, stir, and cook 5 minutes.
3. Add the tomatoes, stock, Italian seasoning, pasta, salt, and pepper, stir, cover, and cook on the Soup setting for 4 minutes.
4. Release the pressure fast, uncover, add the beans, basil, and spinach.
5. Add more salt and pepper, if needed, divide into bowls, add the cheese on top, and serve.

Nutritional Value Per Serving:
Calories: 110
Fat: 2
Carbs: 18
Protein: 5

Zesty Chickpea, Sweet Potato Stew

Prep time: 10 minutes
Cooking Time: 10 minutes
Servings: 2

Ingredients:
- ½ lb. diced sweet potatoes
- ½ lb. chickpeas
- 1 cup orange juice
- 1 cup of water
- 1 cup sliced onion
- Cooking oil spray

Directions:
1. Lightly spray the Instant Pot with a spritz of cooking oil spray.
2. Add the onions and sauté for 5 minutes.
3. Stir in the other ingredients and properly secure the lid.
4. Manually set the timer to 5 minutes on high.
5. Natural-release the steam for about 10 minutes then quick-release and serve.

Nutritional Value Per Serving:
Calories: 240
Fat: 8 g
Carbs: 25 g
Protein: 8 g

Mushroom Lamb Stew

Prep time: 10 minutes
Cooking Time: 35 minutes
Servings: 2
Ingredients:
- tomatoes, chopped
- carrots, sliced
- ½ pound lamb, bone-in
- ½ pound mushrooms, sliced
- 1 tsp. vegetable oil

Directions:
1. Press the sauté cooking function on your Instant Pot; add the oil and heat it.
2. Add the meat and stir-cook until it turns evenly brown, about 10 minutes.
3. Add other Ingredients, stir the mix, and properly close the top lid.
4. Press "meat/stew" cooking function; set pressure level to high and configure cooking time to 25 minutes.

5. After cooking time is over, press "cancel" setting.
6. Quick-release pressure and slowly open the lid, take out the cooked meat and shred it.
7. Add the shredded meat back to the potting mix and stir to mix well.
8. Serve warm.

Nutritional Value Per Serving:
Calories: 324
Fat: 4 g
Carbs: 4 g
Protein: 16 g

Kale Sausage Stew

Prep time: 15 minutes
Cooking Time: 10 minutes
Servings: 2
Ingredients:
- 1lb cooked chopped sausage
- 1lb shredded kale
- 1 cup vegetable broth
- 1tbsp mixed herbs
- 1tbsp gravy

Directions:
1. Mix all the ingredients in your Instant Pot.
2. Cook on Stew for 10 minutes.
3. Release the pressure naturally.

Nutritional Value Per Serving:
Calories: 300
Carbs: 9
Fat: 20
Protein: 30

Chapter 7: Rice Recipes

Mixed Rice Meal

Prep time: 6 minutes
Cooking Time: 20 minutes
Servings: 4

Ingredients:
- cups mixture of brown rice and white rice
- 1½ tsps. salt
- 4½ cups water
- tbsps. olive oil

Directions:
1. Add all the ingredients to the pot.
2. Lock the lid. Select the Multigrain mode, then set the timer for 20 minutes at Low Pressure.
3. Once the timer goes off, do a natural pressure release for 10 minutes, then release any remaining pressure. Carefully open the lid.
4. Check if the grains are soft and cooked well. If not, cook for 5 minutes more.

5 Fluff the mixture with a fork and serve.

Nutritional Value Per Serving:
Calories 126
Carbs 18g
Fat 5g
Protein 0g

Basmati Rice

Prep time: 2 minutes;
Cooking Time: 6 minutes
Servings: 4

Ingredients:
- 2 cups Indian basmati rice
- 2 cups water

Directions:
1 Add the rice and water to the Instant Pot.
2 Lock the lid. Select the Rice mode, then set the timer for 6 minutes at Low Pressure.
3 Once the timer goes off, do a natural pressure release for 3 to 5 minutes. Carefully open the lid.
4 Use a fork to fluff the rice, then serve.

Nutritional Value Per Serving:
Calories 130

Fat 0.2g
Carbs 28.7g
Protein 2.4g

Mexican Rice

Prep time: 6 minutes
Cooking Time: 10 minutes
Servings: 4

Ingredients:
- cups long-grain rice
- 2½ cup water
- ½ cup green salsa
- 1 cup cilantro
- 1 avocado
- Salt and pepper, to taste

Directions:
1. Add the rice and water to the Instant Pot.
2. Lock the lid. Select the Rice mode, then set the timer for 5 minutes at Low Pressure.

3. Once the timer goes off, do a natural pressure release for 3 to 5 minutes. Carefully open the lid.
4. Fluff rice and let it cool. Put the salsa, cilantro, and avocado in a blender.
5. Pulse the ingredients together until they are creamy and mix into the rice.
6. Mix everything together and season with salt and pepper.
7. Serve immediately.

Nutritional Value Per Serving:
Calories 250
Fat 1.3g
Carbs 25.8g
Protein 2.8g

Multigrain Rice

Prep time: 2 minutes
Cooking Time: 20 minutes
Servings: 6 to 8
Ingredients:
- tbsps. olive oil
- 3¾ cups water
- cups wild brown rice

- Salt, to taste

Directions:
1. Combine the oil, water, and brown rice in the pot.
2. Season with salt.
3. Lock the lid. Select the Multigrain mode, then set the timer for 20 minutes on Low Pressure.
4. Once the timer goes off, do a natural pressure release for 5 minutes. Carefully open the lid.
5. Fluff the rice with a fork.
6. Serve immediately.

Nutritional Value Per Serving:
Calories 160
Fat 1.5g
Carbs 33.0g
Protein 5.0g

Raisin Butter Rice

Prep time: 3 minutes
Cooking Time: 12 minutes
Servings: 4
Ingredients:
- cups wild rice, soaked in water overnight and drained
- cups water
- ½ cup raisins
- ¼ cup salted butter
- 1 tsp. salt

Directions:
1. Add all the ingredients to the Instant Pot.
2. Lock the lid. Select the Rice mode, then set the timer for 12 minutes at Low Pressure.
3. Once the timer goes off, perform a natural release for 8 to 10 minutes.
4. Carefully open the lid and use a fork to fluff the rice.
5. Serve warm.

Nutritional Value Per Serving:
Calories 271
Fat 3.0g
Carbs 58.1g
Protein 2.4g

Chapter 8: Pasta Recipes

Zucchini Pasta

Prep time: 10 minutes
Cooking time: 20 minutes
Servings: 5
Ingredients:
- 15 ounces zucchini noodles
- 1 yellow onion, chopped
- garlic cloves, minced
- 12 mushrooms, sliced
- 1 shallot, chopped
- A pinch of basil, dried
- A pinch of oregano, dried
- A pinch of salt and black pepper
- 1 tablespoon olive oil
- 1 cup veggie stock

- cups water
- ounces tomato paste
- 2 tablespoons coconut aminos

Directions:
1. Set your instant pot on Sauté mode, add oil, heat it up, add shallot, garlic, onion, a pinch of salt and pepper, stir and cook for 4 minutes.
2. Add mushrooms, basil and oregano, stir and cook 1 more minute.
3. Add veggie stock, water, tomato paste and aminos, stir, cover and cook on High for 5 minutes
4. Divide zucchini noodles on plates, add mushroom mix on top and serve.

Nutritional Value Per Serving:
Calories 263
Fat 5.2 g
Carbs 11.5 g
Protein 12 g

Pork Pasta

Prep time: 14 minutes.
Cooking: 16 minutes on Stew.
Servings: 4

Ingredients:
- 1 lb lean ground pork
- 1 package pasta, to serve 4
- cups tomato puree
- 1 Tbsp red wine
- Salt and black pepper to taste

Directions:
1. Set Instant Pot on high. Add 1 tablespoon of oil.
2. Add the pork. Season with salt and pepper. Brown 10 minutes.
3. Add the wine. Cook another minute.
4. Add the remaining ingredients. Cook on Stew for 6 minutes.
5. Release the pressure naturally. Let it rest 5 minutes before serving.

Nutritional Value Per Serving:
Calories 200
Fat 4.5 g
Carbs 8.5 g
Protein 10g

Cauliflower with Pasta

Prep time: 10 minutes
Cooking time: 10 minutes
Servings: 4
Ingredients:
- tablespoons butter
- cups cauliflower florets
- garlic cloves, peeled and minced
- 1 cup chicken stock
- Salt, to taste
- 2 cups spinach, chopped
- 1 pound fettuccine noodles
- 2 green onions, chopped
- 1 tablespoon gorgonzola cheese, grated
- sundried tomatoes, chopped
- Balsamic vinegar

Directions:
1. Set the Instant Pot on Sauté mode, add the butter, and melt it. Add the garlic, stir, and cook for 2 minutes.

2. Add the stock, salt, and cauliflower, stir, cover, and cook on the Manual setting for 6 minutes. Release the pressure for 10 minutes, transfer the cauliflower to a blender, and pulse well.
3. Add the spinach and green onions and stir. Heat up a pot with some water and a pinch of salt over medium-high heat, bring to a boil, add the pasta, cook according to instructions, drain, and divide among plates.
4. Add the cauliflower sauce, cheese, tomatoes, and a splash of vinegar on top, toss to coat, and serve.

Nutritional Value Per Serving:
Calories: 160
Fat: 5
Carbs: 23
Protein: 13

Beef and Pasta Casserole

Prep time: 10 minutes
Cooking time: 20 minutes
Servings: 4

Ingredients:
- 17 ounces pasta
- 1 pound ground beef
- 13 ounces mozzarella cheese, shredded
- 16 ounces tomato puree
- 1 celery stalk, chopped
- 1 yellow onion, peeled and chopped
- 1 carrot, peeled and chopped
- 1 tablespoon red wine
- tablespoons butter
- Salt and ground black pepper, to taste

Directions:
1. Set the Instant Pot on Sauté mode, add the butter and melt it.
2. Add the carrot, onion, and celery, stir, and cook for 5 minutes.
3. Add the beef, salt and pepper, and cook for 10 minutes. Add the wine, stir and cook for 1 minute. Add the pasta, tomato puree, and water to cover pasta, stir, cover and cook on the Manual setting for 6 minutes.

4 Release the pressure, uncover the Instant Pot, add the cheese, stir, divide everything among plates, and serve.

Nutritional Value Per Serving:
Calories: 182
Fat: 1
Carbs: 31
Protein: 12

Tuna Pasta

Prep time: 10 minutes
Cooking Time: 40 minutes
Servings: 4
Ingredients:
- 15 oz canned tomatoes
- ½ oz canned tuna
- 2 cups pasta
- 2 garlic cloves
- 2 teaspoons dried basil or oregano

Directions:
1 Set the Instant pot to Sauté and mince in the garlic with some oil to begin cooking.
2 Add in the pasta and tomatoes.
3 Stir in the dried herbs.

4. Add in around 1 cup of water, maybe a little more, until the liquid has just covered the top of the pasta.
5. Set to High Pressure for 6 minutes and then naturally release.
6. Drain the tuna and stir it through the pasta.

Nutritional Value Per Serving:
Calories: 530
Fat: 33.5g
Protein: 32g
Carbs: 5.5g

Chapter 9: Dessert Recipes

Cauliflower Rice Pudding

Prep time: 5 minutes
Cooking time: 14 minutes
Servings: 6
Ingredients:
- 1 tablespoon ghee
- ounces cauliflower, riced
- ounces water
- 16 ounces almond milk
- tablespoons stevia
- 1 egg
- 1 tablespoon coconut cream
- 1 teaspoon vanilla
- Cinnamon to the taste

Directions:

1. Set your instant pot on Sauté mode, add ghee, melt it, add cauliflower rice and stir well.
2. Add water, milk and stevia, stir, cover and cook on High for 8 minutes.
3. In a bowl, mix cream with vanilla and eggs and stir well.
4. Pour some of the liquid from the pot into the egg mixture, stir and add this to the pot, cover and cook on High for 4 minutes more.
5. Divide into bowls, sprinkle cinnamon all over and serve.
6. Enjoy!

Nutritional Value Per Serving:
Calories 172
Fat 2
Carbs 3
Protein 6

Chocolate Dessert

Prep time: 5 minutes
Cooking time: 2 minutes
Servings: 4

Ingredients:
- 2 cups water
- 3.5 ounces dark chocolate, chopped
- 3.5 ounces coconut milk

Directions:
1. In a ramekin, mix chocolate with coconut milk and whisk well.
2. Put the water in your instant pot, add the steamer basket, add ramekin inside, cover and cook on High for 2 minutes.
3. Stir chocolate mix well and serve.
4. Enjoy!

Nutritional Value Per Serving:
- Calories 110
- Fat 3
- Carbs 4
- Protein 2

Tapioca Pudding

Prep time: 10 minutes
Cooking time: 10 minutes
Servings: 4
Ingredients:
- 1 ½ cups water
- 1/3 cup tapioca pearls
- 1 ¼ cup coconut milk
- Zest from ½ lemon
- 3 tablespoons stevia

Directions:
1. Put tapioca pearls in a heat proof bowl, add milk, ½ cup water, lemon zest and stevia and stir well.
2. Put 1 cup water in your instant pot, add the steamer basket, add the dish with tapioca pudding, cover and cook on High for 10 minutes.
3. Divide into dessert cups and serve.

Nutritional Value Per Serving:
Calories 162
Fat 4
Carbs 3
Protein 3

Great Pears Dessert

Prep time: 10 minutes
Cooking time: 10 minutes
Servings: 4
Ingredients:
- 4 pears
- Zest and juice from 1 lemon
- 26 ounces natural grape juice
- 11 ounces natural and Paleo currant jelly
- 4 cloves
- ½ vanilla bean
- 4 peppercorns
- 2 rosemary sprigs

Directions:

1. Put currant jelly in your instant pot, add grape juice, orange zest and juice, cloves, peppercorns, rosemary and vanilla bean and stir well.
2. Dip pears in this mix and wrap them in tin foil.
3. Put the steamer basket into the pot, add wrapped pears inside, cover and cook on High for 10 minutes.
4. Unwrap pears, divide them between plates, drizzle juices from the pot all over and serve.

Nutritional Value Per Serving:
Calories 182
Fat 3
Carbs 2
Protein 3

Sweet Apples

Prep time: 10 minutes
Cooking time: 10 minutes
Servings: 6
Ingredients:
- 6 apples
- 1 cup natural red grape juice
- ¼ cup raisins
- 1 teaspoon cinnamon powder
- 2 tablespoons stevia

Directions:
1. Put the apples in your instant pot, add grape juice, raisins, cinnamon and stevia, toss a bit, cover and cook on High for 10 minutes.
2. Divide among small dessert plates and serve.

Nutritional Value Per Serving:
Calories 130
Fat 1
Carbs 6
Protein 1

Conclusion

Thanks to the Instant Pot, the modern-day cooking has been improved greatly. It is a multipurpose appliance that is helpful in many ways.
Use your Instant Pot to make each and every recipe in the book and you will love every bit of the outcome.
Thank you.

www.ingramcontent.com/pod-product-compliance
Lightning Source LLC
LaVergne TN
LVHW081550270125
802297LV00009B/351